The Science of Living Things

What is the
Animal Kingdom?

A Bobbie Kalman Book

Crabtree Publishing Company

The Science of Living Things Series
A Bobbie Kalman Book

For Ernest,
with my own two hands

Editor-in-Chief
Bobbie Kalman

Writing team
Bobbie Kalman
Greg Nickles

Managing editor
Lynda Hale

Editors
Niki Walker
Jacqueline Langille

Computer design
McVanel Communications Inc.
Lynda Hale
Nancy Twerdohlib

Production coordinator
Hannelore Sotzek

Photographs
John Cancalosi/Tom Stack & Associates: page 23 (bottom)
David Gilchrist: pages 9 (top), 10
The National Audubon Society Collection/Photo Researchers:
  S.L. & J.T. Collins: page 21 (bottom)
  Jany Sauvanet: page 21 (top)
Jeanne White/Photo Researchers: page 11 (top)
Other photographs by Digital Stock and Digital Vision

Illustrations
Barbara Bedell: pages 6-7, 9, 10, 16, 20-21, 26-27

Consultant
K. Diane Eaton, Hon. B.Sc., B.A.
Brock University

Printer
Worzalla Publishing Company

Color separations and film
Dot 'n Line Image Inc.
CCS Princeton (cover)

Crabtree Publishing Company

350 Fifth Avenue
Suite 3308
New York
N.Y. 10118

360 York Road, RR 4,
Niagara-on-the-Lake,
Ontario, Canada
L0S 1J0

73 Lime Walk
Headington
Oxford OX3 7AD
United Kingdom

Cataloging in Publication Data
Kalman, Bobbie
  What is the animal kingdom?

(The science of living things)
Includes index.

ISBN 0-86505-877-6 (library bound)   ISBN 0-86505-889-X (pbk.)
This book introduces the animal kingdom, showing and describing the main
groups of animals and discussing their anatomy, habitats, reproduction, and
classification.

1. Zoology—Juvenile literature. [1. Animals. 2. Zoology.] I. Title. II. Series:
Kalman, Bobbie. The science of living things.

QL49.K295 1997   j590   LC 97-39873
                                                        CIP

Contents

What is an animal?

What do you think of when you imagine an animal? Many people picture something furry with four legs and a tail. Some animals do have fur, but others have smooth skin. Many have legs, but some have none. Some do not have a brain or even a head! Some animals are huge, and others are tiny. There are millions of kinds of animals living all over the world. They live in water, on land, underground, and in the air.

Animal characteristics

Animals may look different from one another, but they are alike in these ways:

- They must eat plants or other animals.
- They must breathe.
- All animals **reproduce**, or make babies.
- They use their senses to find out about the world around them.
- Most animals can move their body.

(left) Praying mantises eat other insects. Their front legs are often folded in a praying position.

What is a kingdom?

A kingdom is group of living things that share basic characteristics. All animals belong to the **animal kingdom**. This book describes the many types of animals that make up this kingdom.

(right) Some animals, such sea fans, look like plants.
(below) Unlike these cheetahs, most animals do not have fur or four legs.

Kingdoms of living things

There are millions of living things in our world. Scientists place them into kingdoms to make them easier to study. Most scientists think there are five kingdoms: **monera**, **protista**, **fungi**, **plant**, and **animal**.

Made up of cells

All living things are made up of one or more **cells**. Cells are alive. They take in food, grow, and split in two to make new cells. They are so tiny that they can be seen only under a microscope.

1. Kingdom monera

The simplest living things such as bacteria and blue-green algae belong to the kingdom monera. They are very small— many are a single cell.

bacteria

2. Kingdom protista

Protists are also tiny and often made of just one cell. Living things such as amoebae and green algae belong to the kingdom protista.

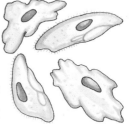

amoebae and paramecia

3. Kingdom fungi

Molds, mushrooms, yeasts, and other fungi belong to this kingdom. Fungi get their food from both living and dead things.

4. The kingdom of plants

Plants are living things with roots, leaves, and stems. They can make their food from sunlight. Many plants have flowers.

5. The animal kingdom

The main kinds of animals are shown here. Most animals are **invertebrates**, or animals without a backbone. The animals on the top half of this page are invertebrates.

Sponges are the simplest animals. (see page 8)

Coelenterates are made up of a stomach and tentacles. (see page 9)

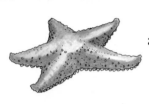

Echinoderms have a body made of five or more identical parts. (see page 9)

Mollusks have tentacles or a shell. (see pages 12-13)

Arthropods have their skeleton on the outside of their body. (see pages 14-15)

Worms have a long, thin body. (see pages 10-11)

Vertebrates are animals with a backbone. The animals on the bottom half of this page are all vertebrates.

Fish live and breathe underwater. (see pages 24-25)

Amphibians live on land and in water. (see pages 20-21)

Reptiles have scaly skin. (see pages 22-23)

Birds have feathers. Most birds fly. (see pages 24-25)

Mammals make milk to feed their babies. (see pages 26-27)

Simple animals

Many kinds of animals have very simple bodies. Some look more like plants than animals! Sponges, coelenterates, and echinoderms are three different groups of simple animals. None of the creatures in these groups has a head, brain, or senses of smell, taste, sight, and hearing. Many cannot move from place to place.

Sponges

Sponges are the simplest animals. They grow underwater in different sizes, shapes, and colors. They have a flexible skeleton. Many of the sponges people use for bathing, housecleaning, or washing their car are actually sponge skeletons.

Staying alive

Sponge babies, or **larvae**, swim around to find a rock or other hard surface on which to live. They attach their body to it and grow into adults. An adult sponge cannot move. To get food, it sucks in water through holes in its body. The water contains bits of food. The sponge strains the food bits from the water and eats them.

Some sponges are barrel-shaped, some are flat, and others are round. This Caribbean sponge looks like a group of pillars.

A sponge sucks in water and food through these holes.

Coelenterates

Coelenterates live underwater. Their body is made up mostly of tentacles and a stomach. The tentacles catch small animals. They sting prey with poison to paralyze them. The stomach then **digests** the food, or breaks it down into energy.

Most coelenterates, such as coral polyps, sea fans, and sea anemones, live in one place. Like sponges, their body is attached to a rock or other hard surface. Jellyfish, on the other hand, swim through the water.

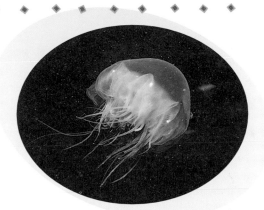

Like other coelenterates, this jellyfish has no skeleton.

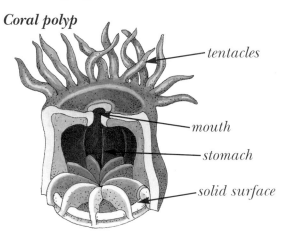

Coral polyp

tentacles

mouth

stomach

solid surface

Each of this sea star's five arms is identical. The mouth and tube feet are on the underside of the animal.

Echinoderms

An echinoderm's body has five or more identical parts. These parts are joined at the center of the body, around the mouth. Small, hollow **tube feet**, usually located on the creature's underside, find and collect food and help the echinoderm move along the ocean floor. Sea stars, sea urchins, and sea cucumbers are examples of echinoderms.

Worms

There are hundreds of thousands of different worms. They all have a very long, thin body without a skeleton. Some worms are flat like a piece of ribbon. Others are round. Most are shorter than your finger, but a few kinds are as long as a bus!

Tubeworms live underwater in a shell-like tube.

What are organs?

Simple animals have only a few basic **organs** in their body. Worms and most other animals have many. An organ is a body part that has an important job to do. The **brain** makes sense of what an animal sees, hears, tastes, smells, or feels. It also tells the body when to move. A **heart** pumps blood throughout the body. **Gills** or **lungs** help many animals breathe. The **stomach, intestines,** and other organs digest food.

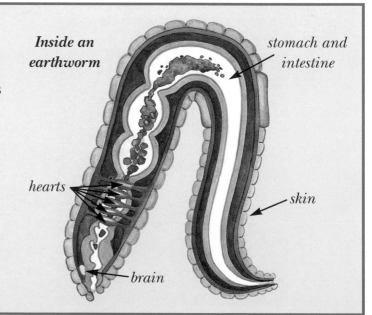

Inside an earthworm

stomach and intestine

hearts

skin

brain

Homes for worms

Some worms live on or under the ground. Others live in water. Many worms are **parasites**. They live on or inside a plant or other animal called a **host**. Parasites feed off their host's body or blood. Sometimes they cause their host to die.

Earthworms live in the ground. When it rains, they surface to keep from drowning in their tunnels.

Cilia and parapodia

Some worms have smooth skin. Many underwater worms are covered with **cilia**. Cilia are tiny body parts that look like feathers or hair. Other worms have leglike **parapodia**. Cilia and parapodia help worms collect food or move.

cilia

Feather duster worms live underwater. They use their feather-like cilia to trap food.

Mollusks

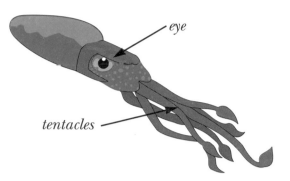

A squid is a mollusk. It has tentacles instead of a foot, and it does not have a shell.

eye

tentacles

Like worms, mollusks have no skeleton. Some mollusks have a shell that protects their soft body. Many have a head with eyes and other sense organs. Most mollusks have a **foot**. This foot does not look like your foot. It is a large, shapeless muscle that helps a mollusk crawl, swim, or burrow. Mollusks are divided into three main groups: **gastropods**, **bivalve mollusks**, and **cephalopods**.

Gastropods

Gastropods are mollusks with a foot that is almost as long as their body. It is under their belly. Snails and slugs are gastropods. They are the only mollusks that can live on land. They crawl along the ground using their foot. Other gastropods such as water snails live underwater and crawl or swim with their foot.

All gastropods except slugs have a spiral-shaped shell. It protects organs such as the heart, stomach, and gills.

shell

foot

Bivalve mollusks

Clams, oysters, and mussels are bivalve mollusks. A bivalve mollusk's body is surrounded by two shells. The shells are joined on one side by a hinge that allows them to open and swing shut. The shells open when the mollusk eats and close to protect it from enemies. Bivalve mollusks use their foot to burrow and sometimes to spring away from danger.

Clams are bivalve mollusks. Their shells open for feeding and close for protection.

Octopuses have excellent eyesight for spotting food and danger.

Cephalopods

Octopuses, squid, and cuttlefish are cephalopods. Cephalopods are the largest invertebrates. They are powerful swimmers that can move quickly. Unlike other mollusks, they do not have a shell on the outside of their body and, instead of a foot, they have many tentacles. Some cephalopods can change color. Some shoot dark liquid into the water to confuse an enemy.

Cephalopods are the most intelligent invertebrates. Scientists have discovered that octopuses, for example, have a good memory and can be taught to perform tricks!

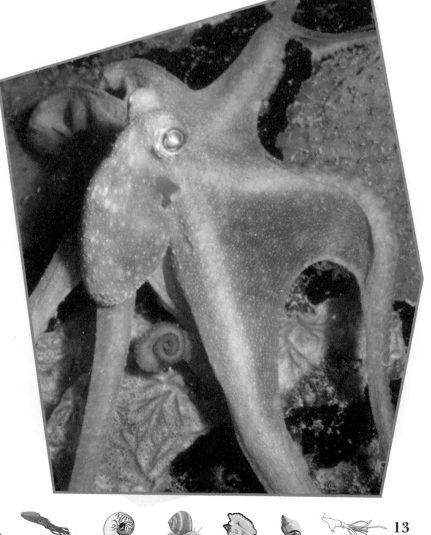

Arthropods

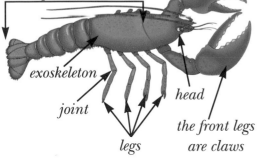

A lobster is a crustacean.

cephalothorax

exoskeleton

joint

legs

head

the front legs are claws

There are more kinds of arthropods in the world than all other kinds of animals put together! The entire outside of an arthropod's body is a hard skeleton called an **exoskeleton**. It covers and protects the soft parts inside the body like a suit of armor. Unlike other invertebrates, arthropods have legs. They can bend them at places called **joints**.

Insects

An insect is an arthropod that has six legs. Its body is divided into a head, thorax, and abdomen. There are millions of kinds of insects. Fleas, ants, flies, bees, and butterflies are just a few groups. Insects live everywhere in the world, including underwater. Many insects have wings. They are the only invertebrates that can fly.

A beetle is an insect.

abdomen

thorax

head

legs

The outside of an arthropod's body is covered by an exoskeleton.

Butterflies have colorful wings. Other winged insects have plain or clear wings.

Arachnids

Arachnids are arthropods with eight legs. Spiders, scorpions, ticks, and mites are arachnids. All spiders and scorpions are **predators**, or hunters. They inject their prey with a poison called **venom**. Mites and ticks are parasites. They feed off the blood of other animals.

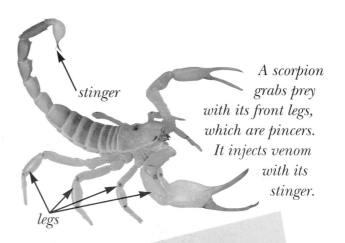

stinger

legs

A scorpion grabs prey with its front legs, which are pincers. It injects venom with its stinger.

Myriapods

Myriapods have more legs than other arthropods. Some have hundreds! Their body has many **segments**, or parts that look similar. Almost every segment has a pair of legs. Centipedes and millipedes are kinds of myriapods.

Crustaceans

Crustaceans are arthropods that live mainly underwater. Different types of crustaceans have different kinds and numbers of legs. Some, such as brine shrimp, have feather-like legs. Crabs and lobsters have ten legs.

A crab's front legs are claws.

How many legs can you count on these millipedes?

Animals with backbones

(above) Frogs and other amphibians are vertebrates.

Most animals are invertebrates. They do not have a **backbone**. A vertebrate is an animal that has a backbone. A backbone is a column of bones along the middle of an animal's back. It supports the rest of the animal's skeleton. Without its backbone, a vertebrate's body would collapse!

backbone

skull

jaw

This is an elephant skeleton. An elephant is a vertebrate. You can see its backbone, skull, jaw, and four limbs.

Cold-blooded and warm-blooded

Almost all animals are **cold-blooded**. The temperature of their blood and body changes when their surroundings become warmer or colder. Only two kinds of vertebrates—birds and mammals—are **warm-blooded**. Their blood and body stay the same temperature no matter how hot or cold their surroundings are. These animals become ill or even die if their body temperature changes very much.

Vertebrate facts

- Most vertebrates have a skeleton made up of bones and cartilage.
- Most vertebrates have two or four limbs.
- Vertebrates have a skull. The skull is a bone that protects the brain.
- Almost all vertebrates have a jaw. The jaw is a bone that helps grab and chew food.
- A vertebrate's brain is much larger than the brain of most invertebrates.
- The largest animals in the world are vertebrates.

The skeleton of elephants and other vertebrates is inside their body. The bones are covered by many layers of muscle, fat, and skin.

Fish

Fish are vertebrates that live in water. Most are cold-blooded. Fish are excellent swimmers. Their skin is covered in tough, smooth scales that help their body slip easily through the water.

Built for swimming

A fish's body is made up mostly of powerful muscles that are used for swimming. Fish swim by moving their body from side to side. Some swim slowly by moving their fins. Most fish, however, use their fins only to steer and keep themselves from rolling onto their side as they swim. Almost all fish have a **swim bladder**, a balloon-like organ that helps them float. When a fish lets air into its swim bladder, its body rises in the water. When it lets in water, its body sinks.

Sharks, skates, rays, and a few other fish have a skeleton made of flexible cartilage. Our ears and the tip of our nose are made of cartilage.

Breathing underwater

Fish have gills that let them breathe underwater. If a fish is taken out of the water, it will die because it cannot breathe. A fish's gills are found on each side of its head. As water passes over the gills, the gills take air from it. To keep water flowing over their gills, fish constantly open and close their mouth. Some sharks swim with their mouth open to move water over their gills.

gills

This butterfly fish and most other fish have a skeleton made up of bones.

Amphibians

An amphibian is a cold-blooded vertebrate that begins its life underwater and moves to land when it becomes an adult. Amphibians have smooth skin that is covered with moist slime called **mucus**. To keep their skin from drying out, most amphibians must live in wet or humid places. Almost all amphibians have a sticky tongue that they use to catch food. There are three main groups of amphibians: **frogs** and **toads**, **salamanders** and **newts**, and **caecilians**.

Frogs and toads have a short body and long, strong hind legs. This amphibian is a tree frog.

From water to land

An amphibian's body changes as it grows from a baby, called a **tadpole**, into an adult. The changes allow the baby to move from its underwater home to one on land. The drawings below show how a great crested newt tadpole grows into an adult.

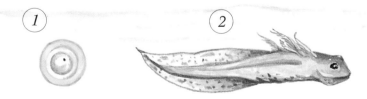

1. An amphibian begins its life as an egg in the water. 2. After a few days, a tadpole hatches from the egg. The tadpole has gills for breathing underwater.

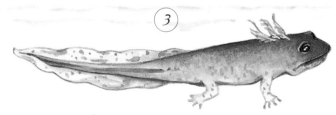

3. The gills shrink as the tadpole starts to grow lungs. Its tail also shrinks and legs begin to grow.

(above) A caecilian has a wormlike body and no legs.

(right) Salamanders and newts such as these eastern newts have short legs and a long body and tail.

④

⑤

4. *The tadpole's lungs replace its gills completely. The tadpole must now swim to the surface of the water to breathe air.*

5. *The tadpole has grown into an adult newt. It now lives on land but visits the water to wet its skin or reproduce.*

snout

Reptiles

Reptiles are cold-blooded vertebrates that have leathery skin covered with scales. They are divided into four main groups: **crocodiles** and **alligators**, **turtles** and **tortoises**, **lizards** and **snakes**, and **tuataras**.

Crocodiles and alligators

Crocodiles and alligators have short legs and a long body covered with bony armor. Their snout is long and filled with pointed teeth for grabbing and holding prey. These reptiles spend most of their time in the water, but sometimes they crawl onto land.

(above) To cool its body, a crocodile holds its mouth open and lets heat escape.

Turtles and tortoises

Turtles and tortoises have short legs and a round, bony shell. They protect themselves from enemies by pulling their legs and head into their shell. Turtles and tortoises may look similar, but there is an easy way to tell them apart— turtles live in water, and tortoises live on land. Some turtles, such as this green turtle, have flippers instead of legs for swimming.

Lizards and snakes

Lizards and snakes have a long body and tail. Almost all lizards have four legs. A few types of lizards, along with snakes, have no legs. Most lizards have rows of pointed teeth with which they grab their prey. Snakes have large fangs that they use to catch prey. Many have hollow fangs that shoot venom. Some inject the venom into prey when they bite.

This cobra shoots a stream of venom to paralyze prey or keep enemies away.

The tuatara

The tuatara looks like a lizard, but it is not. It belongs to its own group. The tuatara is the oldest living type of reptile. Tuataras prefer lower temperatures than other reptiles. They come out only at night, when the air is cool. They live on a few islands near New Zealand.

Birds

Birds are warm-blooded vertebrates. They are the only animals that have feathers. Almost all birds can fly. Birds that fly have hollow bones, unlike the bones of other animals, which are solid.

Feathers

Birds have different types of feathers that do different jobs. The soft, fluffy feathers next to a bird's skin help keep it warm. Outer feathers smooth the bird's body so that it is able to move easily through air or water. The outer feathers also keep water off the bird's skin.

The long, strong feathers on the edges of a bird's wings and tail help the bird get off the ground and steer through the air.

(above) Ostriches and a few other birds cannot fly.

(right) Birds and mammals spend a lot of time caring for their young. They feed their babies and protect them from predators.

A bee eater's beak acts as a tweezer to pluck flying insects out of the air.

Wading birds such as storks need a long beak to find food in water.

A vulture's sharp, hooked beak is ideal for tearing the flesh of prey.

A macaw's hooked beak cracks open nuts and seeds.

Beaks

In order to get off the ground, birds that fly must be lightweight. Their beak may look heavy, but it is made of material that is lighter than bone. This material is also found in human fingernails and toenails.

A bird's beak is an important tool. Birds do most of their work, such as nest-building, cleaning their feathers, and feeding with their beak. Each bird's beak is suited to the type of food it eats. The pictures on this page show some of the different types of beaks.

(above) Some birds, such as this pied kingfisher, have a long, pointed beak for stabbing or grabbing slippery fish.

Mammals

A mammal is a warm-blooded vertebrate. All mammals have some hair or fur on their body. Female mammals make milk to feed to their babies. They are the only animals that are able to do so. Animals from the major groups of mammals are shown here.

(above) Dormice and other **rodents** have long teeth for gnawing food.

(right) This arctic hare and other **lagomorphs** have big ears.

Not hatched from an egg

Many animals begin their life in an egg laid by their mother. When they are well developed, they hatch. Most mammals, however, grow inside their mother's body until they are well developed. They are **live born**, or not hatched from an egg.

Insectivores such as the hedgehog eat insects.

(right) Manatees are one kind of **sirenian**. They live in water and eat plants.

(below) Rhinos and other **perissodactyls** have hoofs and one or three toes.

Elephants are **proboscideans**. They have big ears and a trunk.

Cetaceans such as this orca live in the water. Some hunt prey. Others filter bits of food from the water.

Furry, hairy, and almost hairless

Mammals are the only animals that have hair or fur. Some, such as cats and dogs, are covered with thick, shaggy coats of fur. Fur helps keep mammals warm in cold climates. In hot climates, the fur reflects the sun and keeps the mammal's body cool. Oily fur keeps the skin of water mammals such as beavers and otters from getting wet.

Other mammals, such as dolphins and whales, have only a few hairs on their body. Being almost hairless helps these animals slip easily through water. Whales and dolphins have a thick layer of blubber, so they do not need fur to keep them warm.

Chiropterans, or *bats, can fly.*

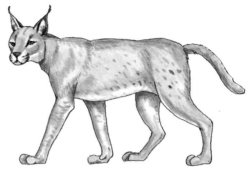

*Cats and other **carnivores** hunt prey.*

*Camels and other **artiodactyls** have hoofs and two or four toes.*

***Primates** such as this mandrill have hands and a large brain.*

*Most **marsupials**, such as koalas, have a pouch to hold their babies.*

*Platypuses are one kind of **monotreme**. Monotremes are the only mammals that lay eggs.*

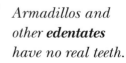

*Armadillos and other **edentates** have no real teeth.*

The shrinking kingdom

All the living things in the world rely on one another for survival. Some animals eat plants, and others eat the plant-eaters. Some break down animal waste, which becomes food for new plants. When one kind of plant or animal disappears from the earth, all the living things that relied on it suffer.

Endangered and extinct

Every day, more animals become **endangered**. When there are only a few of one kind of animal left in the world, that animal is endangered. There are many thousands of endangered animals. They are in danger of becoming **extinct**, or disappearing from our planet forever. Today, humans are usually to blame when an animal becomes endangered or extinct. Humans threaten the survival of animals in many ways.

(opposite page) Elephants are threatened by hunters who take their ivory tusks. People also take away the land on which elephants live.

(below) Tortoiseshell boxes and jewelry are made from the shells of endangered tortoises that are captured and killed by humans.

Hunting

Many animals become endangered because they are hunted by humans. Some are hunted for food. Some such as the black rhino are killed so that parts of their bodies can be used in medicines. Elephants and tortoises are hunted because parts of their body are sold to make expensive jewelry. Many tropical animals, such as parrots, are captured to be sold as pets.

Habitat destruction

Many animals become endangered or extinct when their habitats are changed. Humans change habitats when they cut down trees, set fires, build dams, and drain wetlands. Humans burn and chop down rainforests for lumber and to make way for homes and farms. Some people believe that as many as 200 species of plants and animals are lost for every cleared acre (0.4 hectares) of rainforest.

Pollution

When humans pollute a habitat, all the living things in it are affected. Garbage, farm chemicals, automobiles, factories, mines, and power stations pollute the water, air, and soil. Wildlife that lives in polluted habitats often becomes sick and sometimes dies out. For example, scientists have discovered that some frogs and toads may be especially sensitive to pollution. Many are born missing legs because their parents' bodies were harmed by pollution. Some, such as the golden toad, seem to have disappeared from the wild and may be extinct.

Save the animals!

Many people are trying to save endangered animals. You, too, can help save animals by learning more about them and letting other people know that they are in danger. Avoid buying products that are made from endangered animals. Reduce, reuse, and recycle so that there is less pollution. You can also join a wildlife group that watches and helps animals in your area or around the world.

Water pollution from oil spills, factories, and cities threatens fur seals and other ocean animals.

Words to know

animal kingdom The major group of living things that includes every kind of animal

backbone The column of bones along the middle of a vertebrate's back. The backbone is also called the spine or spinal column.

bone A part of a vertebrate's skeleton; the hard substance of which the parts of a vertebrate's skeleton are made.

cell The most basic part of every living thing; most plants and animals are made of millions of connected cells

characteristic A feature or quality

cold-blooded Describing an animal whose body temperature changes with the temperature of its environment

digest To break down food so that the body can use it for energy

endangered Describing a plant or animal that is in danger of dying out

exoskeleton The hard, shell-like outer skeleton that protects an arthropod's body

extinct Describing a plant or animal that no longer exists

habitat The natural place where a plant or animal is found

host An animal that is attacked by a parasite

invertebrate An animal that has no backbone

larva A baby insect or similar animal after it hatches from an egg. A larva has a soft, wormlike body.

limb A body part such as a leg, arm, or wing

live born Describing a baby animal that is not hatched from an egg

organ A part of the body that does a special job. For example, the heart pumps blood throughout the body.

paralyze To cause an animal to lose power and feeling in parts of or all of its body

parasite A creature that feeds off a living plant or animal's body

predator An animal that kills and eats prey

prey An animal that is hunted and eaten by another animal

reproduce To make babies

scale A small, flat, tough structure on the skin of some animals, such as fish and reptiles.

senses The abilities that help an animal be aware of its surroundings, including sight, hearing, smell, taste, and touch

skeleton The set of bones, rods, shells, or other stiff substances that supports an animal's body

species A group of very similar living things whose offspring can make babies

tentacle A long, flexible body part used for feeling, grasping, and moving

vertebrate An animal that has a backbone

warm-blooded Describing an animal whose body temperature stays the same no matter what the temperature of its environment

Index

1 2 3 4 5 6 7 8 9 0 Printed in the U.S.A. 6 5 4 3 2 1 0 9 8 7